MY
THREE
HUSBANDS

KELLY Y. RAGIN

3G Publishing, Inc.
Loganville, Ga 30052
www.3gpublishinginc.com
Phone: 1-888-442-9637

First published by 3G Publishing, Inc. October, 2019

ISBN: 978-1-941247-61-7

Printed in the United States of America

Contents

For My Girls. My Legacy.
Ericka & Erin

&

In loving memory of my grandmother, Vera Brown, who did not allow one bad apple to spoil the whole barrel.

ACKNOWLEDGEMENTS

Sometimes saying thank you never seems to be enough. When I reflect on my journey, I'm forced to take a deep breath. One might say that I've lived a pretty colorful life. This much is true. However, the many, many life jackets I have are because of the beautiful family and friends God assigned to me. JUST ME. I'm thankful to God for granting me the strength, courage and desire to write this book. I pray that it becomes a game changer for the person who needs to change—the game.

First, I thank you, my graceful and wise Mother. You loved me first. And you gave me one of my first loves. Reading. Thank you for introducing me to the world of reading and writing. I remember the days that you would instruct me to sit with you in my bedroom and read Bible Stories out loud to you. I didn't always want to read, but the more I did, the more the stories became interesting; leaving me ready to take on the next chapter. This was a beautiful gift you gave me; along with being the world's best Mama! I love you!

Next, my heart beats and my "why". I've repeated this sentiment several times but, all that I do, I do for you both. My legacy. I have to truly take this time to thank my daughters. I never set out to have a family business, but I perceive it now as a gift.

To my oldest, Ericka, --your gift of creativity and graphic design still amazes me. Whenever I ask, you always deliver. Thank you for designing my book cover. I was in utter disbelief on how you captured my title in your design. I loved it immediately. Keep striving and working hard "Ricka". Your dream of success is around the corner. I wholeheartedly believe that you can do anything. You never cease to amaze me. I love you!

To Erin, my baby girl. You started out as my Senior editor for this project. You did not hesitate to jump right in on editing and fixin' grammar and punctuations. However, you totally and pleasantly surprised me when your coaching skills kicked in. The Writer's Coach" is what I called you. You challenged me to think past the surface of my purpose. You're truly ready. GO GET IT! Your abilities to shine above the rest are outstanding. I love you!

To my Son-in Love, Erin (yes…I have two Erins now!) thank you. Your mind and creative genius are simply brilliant. You've been in the "Family Business" from day one and you have truly been the catalyst in jump starting the visual senses of what I could not do on my own. Your mind is genius. I Love you.

To all of my close family and friends, near and far— Thank You! Thank you for listening and for "holding it down" when I didn't have the strength to do it on my own. True Friends—the ones who never judged. The ones who prayed in my absence instead of whispering.

The friends who showed up just because. True Friends. My Tribe. My True Blues. I Love You.

To Shawn, my cousin-sister. For being the listening ear all of my life. For the advice I valued and even for the advice I didn't. Somehow, very much like a big sister, you've always given me support and your presence. I have no words to capture my appreciation for your loyalty. I love you.

To "My Three Husbands" – Thank you for being you. I've truly learned to embrace every inch of my experience and journey of love and life with you. I would not be who I am today without my experiences with you. I'm so grateful that God taught me patience, He gave me a heart to love people and He especially taught me about forgiveness and unconditional love. I have Absolutely no regrets. I do wish that my lessons learned were not from pain and hurt, but I recognize that through God's grace, it was the pain that led me to my purpose. I appreciate the opportunity through growth, maturity and understanding to learn that life goes on, people change, and that LOVE prevails. OH…and that God's love is greater than any love I've ever experienced. I laugh sometimes when I think about some of the great moments shared. For example, I learned how to properly fold bath towels. I learned to enjoy dancing with a partner like no one is watching and I learned how to make a dollar stretch to the moon and beyond. So, see. I'm a true witness that there's a light at the end of the tunnel.

INTRODUCTION

Marriage has always been extremely important to me. This book is more than just typical words typed on paper. It's My Life! I struggled with what to specifically share. What NOT to share. However, when I took a peek into the fabric of my journey, I knew immediately that it was more important for me to share the lessons. And I have many. I don't have any claims that give a magic solution or answer to the perfect marriage, but I sincerely believe that I have valuable information from my own personal experiences that will not only bless you, the reader, but will give tools that will assist with building the start of a great relationship and marriage. The title was chosen because, well quite frankly.... I've been married 3 times. There was a time that I would feel humiliation when telling someone that number. I often feared that I would be ridiculed and scoffed at because of it. I worried that my peers would wonder "what's wrong with her". My prayer is that once you've read my story, you will love and gain an appreciation for "My 3 Husbands", as I have done.

At the prompting of husband #3, I received my certification in Life Coaching and chose to put my focus on Relationships. Who better than me, to share tips and lessons learned on how to avoid pitfalls, and how to choose wisely? As I often say....

"I didn't go through all that, for nothing!!"

MARRIAGE #1

Transparency is my Friend....

I was 21 years old when I first jumped the broom. Getting married seemed to be one of the top goals on the list for most young ladies my age. We would day-dream about the type of wedding we wanted even more than the type of husband we needed. I can remember my 16 year-old self, fantasizing about being married. I'd wear my bubble gum machine ring and prance in front of the mirror, flashing my hand back and forth. I suspect that the idea of marriage was like a fairy tale to me; as it is with most young girls. I could envision my wedding colors being lavender and white. I learned from TV shows and movies about the roles of the wedding party. I remember thinking about how cute it would be to have the little girl next door toss lavender and purple flowers down the aisle. Then, my younger cousin, could come skipping down the aisle with a bell yelling, "Here comes the bride! Here comes the bride!". It's interesting how at that age I made up what I believed to be the perfect wedding.

Despite my father dying while I was very young, I never felt that I experienced "Daddy issues". I simply wanted to be married because I always felt that it was a beautiful part of life. My mother re-married when I was 7. My Step-dad stepped in and became my Daddy. He was there for me in a tremendous way. He truly cared for me and raised me and I'm forever grateful that he's still in my life. Nevertheless, the "idea" of marriage was what I desired whether I had a Dad around or not. Marriage was my mission— or so I thought.

While in my 3rd year of college, I chose having a wedding over finishing my education. I had no idea that I was about to become educated by the books of hard knocks. At the time, I was 20 years old. I was a Nursing student at Georgia State University. I was very proud to be in college, because not many in my immediate family had gone. I felt that I was accomplishing something truly great! Until… my PELL grant was not renewed. I could not afford to pay out of pocket, nor could my family afford to obtain big loans. So, I chose to sit out for a year. During that time, I met my first husband. Excited about the thought of being married, independent and living my life as an adult, I told myself that I would finish my degree later. Well, I quickly learned that college might have been easier, because marriage is no joke! I will gladly shout to the roof tops to those who are contemplating marriage to please focus on the MARRIAGE and not the wedding.

Marriage is not about the bachelor and bachelorette parties leading up to the beautiful venue, décor, delicious red velvet cake, the gorgeous gown and tux, or even that all-inclusive trip to the Fiji Islands. It's about standing on the vows of which you promise one another before God and family. Marriage is about EV-

ERYTHING that Corinthians 1:13 speaks of.. like love being patient, kind, and long suffering.

When I reflect on my first marriage, I always have a spirit of gratitude. If a person never takes the lessons learned, he or she will always remain stuck. Though my marriage didn't work, we remained in our union for almost twenty years! I often say that we grew up together because technically… we did. We were both young and finding our way.

As I reflect, I recognize that I rushed into marriage for a few reasons. During that time, I felt that my mother's rules were too strict, (although today, I would beg to differ). I was eager to leave home and experience the "adult life". I wanted to have my own apartment, not have a curfew, and make my own decisions. Unbelievably, I thought that these things made me "grown". Many years later, I gasp at the silliness of my decision-making skills at that age. If there's one thing for sure, it's that marriage made me into the woman I am today. I learned so much from "Ricky". I decided very early that I would never have the man-bashing party. See…that's the easy part. With age comes maturity and growth. Of course, there were other things that occurred in the marriage that influenced my decision to divorce--but those are not up for discussion in this book.

Marrying another human being comes with the whole enchilada! And sometimes that may include heartburn.

Because I was still so young, the marriage felt like a life sentence after a while. In saying that, I mean that I had not figured out my own life or even lived my life. But yet and still, we held on. I gained two of my biggest fans, my heart throbs, and my reason for living-- My two beautiful daughters. It was really important to me to allow my girls the opportunity to grow up in a family with both parents. I wanted them to feel whole. I didn't want them to come from a broken home. Interestingly enough, I learned that it was more important for me to show them that having peace as an individual trumped what society defined as happiness. I always hope that every piece I write, somehow will get into their hands (by choice!). Especially this one!

Once my daughters became young adults, I always encouraged them to take their time in dating and to not be in a hurry. I believe that this is truly my Number 1 lesson learned. As you continue reading, you're going to see how that all unfolds.

MARRIAGE #2

Second Chances.....

After coming out of my first marriage of almost twenty years, I immediately went into the "It's All About Me" phase. I was determined that from here on out, I would be doing things my way...and my way only. See, I felt manipulated and controlled for many years. I didn't feel that I had a voice, and I felt that I lost control. Not to bash, but I would guess that people put onto you what's been placed onto them. "Ricky" was acting out what he experienced. Who knows? Ultimately, we grew together and had a beautiful family. Nevertheless, over time it became obvious that we were no longer compatible. This newly divorced young woman was not about to let that be her story, ever again... or so I thought.

With this new revelation, I was on a new mission. I enjoyed the dating scene for what it was worth, but having been married for almost twenty years, marriage was all that I knew. I was simply comfortable with companionship; good or bad. Of course, my girlfriends urged me to enjoy the single life. I did for a little while. It was fun, exciting, and was always an adventure meeting new people and doing different activities.

During this time, I had taken on a new position in my career in the area of HIV/AIDS as a Public Health Analyst. Being in this environment for forty plus hours a week exposed me to various organizations and people of all walks of life. It also opened my eyes to the tragedy and downfall that the virus and disease has on the lives of so many beautiful people. I became so involved and knowledgeable that it changed my life and view on dating and relationships. This certainly encouraged me to want to marry again. Quickly! Dating became scary to me because I already knew the rules. Society creates this picture that being free to love and explore in sexuality is acceptable. As a single woman, the rules that I had been taught were to abstain from fornication, etc. Abstaining during that time, was not my idea of fun or living my best life. However, the importance of being in a committed relationship was even more apparent to me. At that time and age, I wasn't convinced that abstaining was the way to go.

When I met my second husband, who we will call "Denzel", I was excited to meet someone who was warm hearted, sensitive, extremely caring and appeared to be extremely devout to God. Most important to me; he didn't make a fuss about me, "doing me". I really thought… "Wow, I hit the jack pot!". Thing is, I didn't date him long enough to see some of the other characteristics that would prove to be vital for the survival of our marriage. I needed traits like consistency, commitment, passion, dedication to marriage, valuing the role of being a husband and taking financial responsibility. At this point, I thought attracting someone who appeared to be the opposite of "Ricky" would make all the difference. I quickly learned what Grandma meant when she said… "Love don't pay the rent".

After 5 years, I could see and feel that "Denzel" was not ready for true commitment in our marriage. He cared for me deeply; which made dissolving the marriage challenging. In my opinion, he was not content with his own life. Therefore, there was not much of anything he could offer to me as my husband. We were simply companions who cared for each other. I had to become real with myself. I learned what true love really means.

Divorce is never something that most people contemplate when getting married. But sometimes, circumstances force you to make decisions that are necessary.

Marriage #3

"What's Love Got to do with it?"

After having gone through two other failed marriages, I thought that it was over for me. I could not imagine saying to someone... "I'm on my 3rd marriage". How humiliating! My immediate thought is that I would instantly be judged before anyone knew my story. In today's world, society would rather believe what sounds fascinating than believe the truth. Nevertheless, with all of my pride, yes, I married for a 3rd time. Humiliated? Not so much. God holds the blue print and has different plans for our lives than we could ever imagine. Love is more than an emotion. Love is a verb. Love requires action and putting your feet to your faith. So, to answer the question, love has EVERYTHING to do with it.

As much as I wanted to be completely done with love, God showed me that He held the deed to my heart. He showed me that He could use my pain for HIS purpose. Though I decided that I was over the whole "love and marriage" piece, my heart would not allow it. I first had to learn about SELF LOVE. Once I gained a better handle on "loving me", I was able to open my heart to the possibility of taking on a new mate. When you learn to love yourself, you make your

self a priority. You look at life with a different set of lenses and your view becomes crystal clear.

In my 3rd marriage, "Maurice" and I made a conscious decision that we wanted a committed "Partner for life". We were done with the dating life but wanted more. We had similar values and goals that lined up, like spending time with family, focusing on our health, traveling, and exploring business ventures. This time, I married for PURPOSE. I focused on the person—and nothing else. Do we experience issues in our relationship? Of course, we do. However, this time I am equipped and enlightened on what it takes to make love work and to have a successful relationship and marriage.

This book was inspired by true life experiences. One sure fact is that, YES-- I've had 3 husbands. I guess the humiliation paid off. But most importantly, I've learned not to waste my pain. The pain is what brought wisdom. Here are my lessons learned.

LOVE LESSON 1
Before Saying I DO. Pump The Breaks!

During my dating season, I remember going on date, after date, after date-- praying and asking God this one question: "Is he my husband?" I always wondered if I was encountering the man who was pre-destined to be my husband. This is why it's so important to have a personal relationship with God so that you know when He actually answers. Often times, I would think that I saw a "sign". I would question it over and over again. When God is truly in the mix, you will know without a shout of a doubt.

PUMP YOUR BREAKS!! Slow down. Or slow him or her down. Don't become so consumed with flattering words, smiles or good looks. Beauty fades.

I would say, by far that this is the most valuable lesson learned. Develop a personal relationship with God through prayer. Then, seek God's approval first. In all of your decisions, always ask God to intervene, while you're waiting on your answers. There's power in waiting. Plus, it's worth the wait! Rushing ruins. So, let Love happen.

"Sit still, until God REVEALS".

--The LovePreneur

When you are unsure of something, take a breather. Rest on it. I promise the answer will reveal itself. I took 1 year to study and research this thing called love. I made it a priority because it's an important subject in my life. I made several sacrifices, experienced my own personal challenges but I also overcame a lot of those challenges as well. Learning to "BE STILL" was hard for me. At one point, God had to force me to BE STILL. I sat in the hospital for what most would think was a minor medical issue. However, medical terminology would have me "sitting/laying" in a hospital bed for 3 days. What an amazing time of reflection. I encourage you to own your time, and take your time before you are forced to make time.

One of my favorite virtual counselors [RC Blake; Los Angeles, CA] offered some excellent advice on the 10 Common mistakes that women make with men. Here are my sentiments on that advice:

1. Don't tell everything too soon. We as women tend to share ALL of our business from the jump! Hold some of the gravy for later AFTER you receive confirmation that he (or she) deserves to know more. It's a beautiful thing when you can share you heart with the person you marry.

2. Don't forget to call Uncle Junior! There's absolutely nothing wrong with taking your new guy/ or lady to meet a trusted relative or friend. Sometimes they can see characteristics we don't. Naturally, it's your call to make the final cut. But it

truly is no harm in having another set of eyes to check out what you might miss.

3. Don't forget your heart. Not taking time to heal wounds from previous or broken relationships.

4. Don't use your body. Forgo the plan to draw a person to you by using sex. You will immediately set the tone for the potential relationship….and it may not be favorable.

5. Don't psyche yourself out. Dismiss the idea that you can change a person to suit your ideal relationship.

6. Don't accept or tolerate abuse in any form. Emotional or physical.

7. Don't take advice from women in your circle who have never been married. Yes, they could still offer some great relationship tools but it's best to confide in like-minded women. Married or women in serious relationships.

8. Don't put your dreams on the top shelf for the other person. Resentment will build towards them sooner or later.

9. Don't give passes. Don't accept the fact that the other person can NEVER accept responsibility or simply admit if he was "wrong".

10. Don't keep silent by not asking questions. Jot them down prior to meeting up. The more questions you ask, the more you learn about your potential mate. As a matter of fact, his/her answers will prove later if he or she is an honest person.

Proverbs 3; 5-7
"Trust in the Lord with all thine heart and lean not to thine own understanding. In All Thy ways, Acknowledge Him, and He shall direct thy path. Be not wise in thine own eyes".

LOVE LESSON 2
Know Thyself. Love Thyself.

I will be completely transparent here. In all 3 marriages, I did NOT take enough time to really get to know my mates during the dating phase. I got caught up in the euphoria and infatuation of the newness of the relationship. And as much as this is truly important, --learning and knowing THYSELF FIRST, is the first step on this journey. During a period of my singleness, I took advantage of my free time. I have 2 daughters, so I tried to spend as much time as I could with them in their activities. I stepped up my servitude and became more active in my church. I chose organizations that were of true interest to me versus being recruited to fill a vacancy. This is when I learned the importance of really taking time for yourself. Sure—I had girlfriends, but this was during a time when I had to learn on my own. Creating a personal private space is vital; because you will most certainly have times where you'll need to just steal-away. Having personal space allows you time to talk to God and it also gives you time to HEAR from God! Another thing I did often was treat myself! This included, dinner, movies, concerts and......shopping! When I look back over those days I smile, because many days, I thought I wouldn't make it through. But here I am attesting to how I pushed forward.

How different would I do things today! I would simply, take my time. If a potential partner is pressing you or pushing, you to move too fast…red flag.

Unfortunately, I never paid attention to the red flags. Seems like I was always in a hurry and "for what" I have no idea. To go nowhere.   Truth is, I never viewed it as being in a hurry, but essentially that's what it was… hurriedness. Sometimes, decisions to marry so quickly are based on fear. Fear that if you don't say "I DO" now, then that potential mate may quickly change his/her mind. Well, one thing for sure; YOU DO GET TO CHANGE YOUR MIND. That's the beauty of being a mature and seasoned adult.

If he/she has a changed mind, then that person was not ready! Also, don't be easily persuaded by anyone! I think back on the "Power of Persuasion" from my grandmother. I truly believe that the women of her generation thought "Well, if a man wants to marry you, you'd better say yes…and quickly! or someone else will." This unsounded logic, was passed down generation to generation. No one in my immediate family talked about having patience while dating. No one ever expressed that it was okay to be single. And happy. Heck I didn't discover this until after divorce. Even during a rough patch, I would remind myself of the importance of showing my daughters what it looked like to be happy and single versus married and miserable. I wanted to show them a "Strong mother". I pray that I did.

A person will never know all there is to know about

a person. Only God holds the keys to that safe! Thank goodness! However, there are so many key factors or characteristics to look for that most times are right in your face.

We've all heard the quote: "When a person shows you who they are the first time, BELIEVE THEM". I believe Dr. Maya Angelou empowered us with this one. Ain't that the truth!! Don't ignore this one!! Put in the time. Meaning don't say "I DO" until you have seen and experienced enough of the true character of your beloved mate. It may take 6 months before his/her representative expires—and then the real person just might peek their head in the door!

It's best to be happy and alone than to be miserable in a trapped horrible relationship. Be in love with yourself! Don't give in to someone who feels like they "NEED" you or their world will fall apart. BE CAREFUL!! You don't need a parasite! KNOW YOURSELF! Everyone who smiles at you, is not necessarily for you. Even the elderly gentleman or lady at Walmart gets paid to smile at you. Food for thought, right? In all seriousness, don't allow desperation to creep in and rest on your brain. Take your time and know thyself.

LOVE LESSON 3
Who's this Person?
After the Representative Leaves

If you're anything like me as a woman, you have a list or two. When I was twenty, I had a list that included the type of characteristics I desired in a mate. The things I would like for him to possess, the type of family he would come from, things about his personality that I thought would be great for him....and me. Thing is, I didn't have a REAL clue about what would really be necessary to sustain a marriage. My first list looked a little something like this:

Loves God
Good job
Good family
Tall
Nice smile

That was it. Basic. Plain and simple. To the point. However, many moons later my list changed a great deal.

√   Loves God more than anything in this world.
√   Will respect my daughters as his own children
√   Financial stability; career with excellent benefits

√   Has his own home and car
√   Has excellent hygiene
√   A nice smile and great oral hygiene
√   Loves to kiss.
√   Loves to show and display affection
√   Ambitious
√   Communicate Effectively
√   Non-abusive. Non-Womanizer. 1 woman man.
√   Cherish me. Have eyes ONLY for me.
√   Loves to travel and experience new things….
√   Chemistry and Passion

I hope that you see my point here. With time and growth comes maturity. In time, I saw life differently. My desire changed. My needs changed. So in meeting a potential mate, I find it very imperative that you take time to find out who they really are…to the core. As much as one possibly can. TRUST ME ON THIS.

OBSERVATION is NECESSARY.

People will show you who they really are in their actions. All you need to do is take a little time. Have some patience. Wait. Watch and see for yourself. If he or she tickles your fancy (or other things)….then you have a starting point….and that's all. This is just lesson #3. Keep reading!!

Amos 3:3
"How can two walk, except they agree?"

LOVE LESSON 4
Traits & Characteristics
The Four Seasons

Before I dig into this chapter, it's imperative that I first state that I am not a licensed therapist or clinician. However, I have studied this subject a good bit and will be sharing excellent reference points noted from credible resources.

I'm gonna make this as plain and simple as I possibly can.

If it walks like a duck, then….. If it barks like a dog, then…..

Most of us have heard many quotes and cute sayings all of our lives as it relates to relationships. These are no different.

A person is exactly who they show you they are; in a sense. We should never move into a relationship with thoughts of believing we can change a person. The only person we can change is ourselves. We may be able to manipulate a situation slightly, but we can never change it completely. This is where acceptance becomes an option. Either you accept the person or situation for who they are, or NOT.

There's a scripture in Proverbs 21; 12 that says; *If God chooses not to manipulate a man's heart, what makes you think you can?*

I Love that! Sometimes we fool ourselves into thinking we are just that good! We can NEVER be that good. This is because God gives us all choices. So, it's up to people to choose to change.

I love this quote that says: "If there's a crack in the glass, throw it out. Get a new one".

Not necessarily a profound statement. But it sure does make sense. A glass is fragile. One little knick could become a serious problem. Yes, it seems minor; until you run your hand across the knick and blood is everywhere! OR you pour your favorite beverage, then suddenly it leaks or gushes through the unexpected broken vessel. This statement merely states to me that, no one is perfect. We all have a few knicks and bruises. However, the person who encounters those knicks and bruises will always take a chance. In other words—the glass may or may not break. You decide if you want to keep the glass. Or get a new one!

FOUR SEASONS

A dear friend (Rochelle) shared with me a word from the wise. She said that while dating, this was something that each person should experience—the 4 seasons. Give yourself time as you learn more about yourself....

and your potential mate as well.

Here are the seasons:

How does your potential mate respond:
» When you are ill? Does he/she show empa-thy? Are they nurturing?
» In times of bereavement? When you are grieving? Does he/she show sympathy or concern? Or are they emotionless?
» When there is a crisis? When things are upsetting? Does he/she overreact? Become violent? Shut down? Communicate effec-tively?
» When you achieve? In times of your achievement? Does he/she celebrate you, or show jealousy?

Again, make sure you experience the 4 Seasons. It's very much the same in our every day lives. We have no choice but to weather the storms of life as they come, as well as experieince the beauty of the flowers that bloom in the newness of Spring and enjoy the colorful views of Fall and the changing of the leaves much like changes in our lives. Then finally, bask in the brightness of the sun rays and sunshine during the Summers of your life.

LOVE LESSON 5
Family Values

When dating someone new, it is imperative that you're honest from "jump street". The discussion of family values should happen right away. Putting it off creates a sense of "low priority". No—you're not marrying the person immediately, or maybe not at all, but if this person is "the one", the relationship must start off with truth.

I've witnessed scenarios where one party purposely omitted the number of children he had fathered. The couple continued dating; for quite a while. He did not reveal the truth about his children until they were close to marriage. In this case, the truth crushed his partner. She no longer wanted the relationship.

Another example---a widowed woman, in her mid-40's started to date again after almost 3 years of the passing of her beloved spouse. She cherished their marriage, and especially his memory. Naturally, her children were still grieving the loss of their father as well. He was an awesome dad. To preserve his memory, his urn was kept in a special place in their home. Her partner knew of its importance. They continued dating. He asked her to become his wife. The planning proceeded. Until the urn disappeared. YIKES!!! This was devasting to the family. It was quickly revealed that the fiancé had hidden the urn because he didn't want to take it into their new marriage and new home. INSECURE! DECEIT! DISTRUST! NO LOYALTY! And the list goes on. She canceled the wedding. Regrouped. Ultimately, God sent her a new mate and husband.

Here's one last example:

This one is my very own personal story. Before marrying a 3rd time, I promised myself that IF I ever decided to marry again, I would not have a full wedding. No bells. No whistles. I had done that twice before and I didn't want to deal with all the hoopla. I was older, wiser and more simplistic. Besides, I had also decided that IF I married again, it wouldn't be the lovey-dovey kind. But a partnership of sorts, and that love would not be a key factor. At least not at right away. I'm sure you're wondering why I would not make love a key factor. Well, I thought since I was middle aged, and had been married twice before, that love—perhaps, was overrated. I thought that if I focused more on partnership and how we could both benefit from the marriage, then it had a better chance of surviving. However, I also had one more "biggie" that I never thought would become a "biggie". I decided that I would elope and return already married. My daughters were young adults, my mother had already given her blessing and insisted on coming to the Justice of the Peace with us. I felt that I owed no one anything. Boy was I wrong!

WRONG! DEAD WRONG!

My Three Husbands

When "Maurice" and I married at the Justice of the Peace, my daughters were extremely devastated that I did not include them on this life changing moment. I didn't realize the magnitude that this decision would make. I just figured that since it was not my first marriage, they would be "OK" …and would understand that we would celebrate later. I also, realized too late and after the fact the importance of making sure that FAMILY VALUES were addressed at the onset of my decision to marry. MAJOR LESSON LEARNED! It cost me peace in my family, for weeks.

"Family matter" talks and discussions with a potential partner are vital. It allows the couple an opportunity to share what is deemed most important to them. My daughters were young adults at the time of my 3rd marriage. I just "assumed" they would be ecstatic with my decision. Now---please don't misunderstand: "I'm the boss of me!". They don't dictate my moves. But I do strongly believe that as family, it would have certainly been appropriate to chat about my intentions. Not seeking permission, but to keep the peace.

See, Love has EVERYTHING to do with marriage. This was not a shocker for me, but out of exasperation I tried to convince myself that it did. Trying to deal with challenges in a marriage without God's help is senseless and useless. Especially in blended families. Thankfully, we both had a strong faith in God. And thankfully, my husband had a strong desire and L-O-V-E for me; even when I chose not to love. As my dear friend C. Nicole reminded me, there are no winners in divorce. So make sure you make a solid, God-ordained decision.

So, see. LOVE does prevail.

Within 2 years of marriage, we definitely had our challenges. REALLY BIG ONES! However, through all of the adversity, our love grew stronger and there was no denying it. LOVE HAS EVERYTHING TO DO WITH MARRIAGE!! God's love first. Then, Love-love. No, it's not going to ever be perfect. But we can strive to get close to it. We've learned to actually LISTEN to one another as well as back it up with action. We also wrote a contract to each other. We spelled out EXACTLY what was important to us significantly. OUR TRUST and FAITH in God teaches us to keep believing nothing but the best.

B L E N D E D

Tips to consider when marrying and blending Families:

- *Seek Counsel.*
  This allows you to address major issues BEFORE they arrive. Not all blended families have issues, but a large percentage of them do. Go ahead, get a good jump start!

- *Prioritize.*
  As husband and wife or as an engaged couple, it's going to be important to show the "blended kids" that your union is at the TOP of the list. But yourself in their shoes, and act accordingly!

- *Be consistent.*
  Show consistency in how you manage the family…and family matters.

- *Communicate. Communicate. Communicate!*
  About everything.

This one will NEVER get old…
"A Family That Prays TOGETHER, Stays Together"

LOVE LESSON 6
Does it Line Up?
RED FLAGS

While dating, both parties are paying attention. To EVERYTHING! The truth is, both parties are observing and watching seeking the same answers. What specifically? It varies. It also depends on what you are seeking in a mate. More often than not, the answers are staring you directly in the eyes.

These are called RED FLAGS.

The definition of Red Flag means = A warning. Nothing fancy here. Just plain ole real talk. And truthfully, that's exactly how a red flag will show up. Like a huge warning. Pay close attention to them when they do. A Red Flag is like having a guardian angel. It's sent to you, to protect you.

RED FLAGS WAVE NON-STOP!

I recall during my dating season; a gentleman I was dating showed signs of mental illness. I didn't notice at the start of our dating, but it didn't take long before the signs would show up. Mental illness is SO REAL and not to be taken lightly in the least bit. We all have experienced it in some way. Usually in our families, we dismiss it or disguise it as being "normal" for "That Person". Well, during this brief dating period, initially, things were AWESOME! This guy was a ton of fun and full of energy. This lasted for about 5 months. Continuous fun and excitement. Then the other shoe dropped!

When I look back over this entire fiasco, I couldn't blame anyone but myself. I remember the first time I was invited to his home for dinner. His home was nice, clean and comfortable. He wanted to cook for me. I'm usually a little leery of eating other folks' food, but I made an exception because he was so convincing that he was a great cook. While there, we chatted and watched a movie after dinner. It was getting late, so I started packing up. He insisted that I stay because it started to rain. I insisted, that I leave before the rain got worse. Once I was home, he called. However, his call was not necessarily, a well-check call. He wanted me to know how upset he was that I didn't stay at his home. I explained that I was still getting to know him, and that would have been unacceptable. He became a little irate; more than I was used to experiencing. I didn't care for his "person" after that conversation. NOW. FIRST RED FLAG! I should have taken that to heart and blocked his phone number. I did not. I later learned in counseling that I had a "Need to be needed" and a "Need to fix people". Something that I wish I had addressed in MYSELF in the early days. So after about a week, I called him back to check on him, and to see if he had calmed down. SO FOOLISH OF ME!! See, this is what a person does who is not confident within. At that time, I missed the fun we had, but not realizing that, his particular fun came with a price. Needless to say, with a simple apology and the "I miss you' s" we reconnected and continued dating. I TOTALLY DISMISSED MY RED FLAG!!

After 5 months of dating, and I can only presume, that he had missed a few days of his medication [I did the math and my own investigating] he began to act out in a way I had NEVER EVER experienced in life. It was verbal abuse, and after a while, I could not even identify who he was from the words he spoke to me. It was terrifying! Even worse, it all came out in a roar based on a simple comment I made. Some persons with mental illness are aware that they are ill, but it's difficult for them to discuss. Especially with a new person in their lives. This is completely understandable. This is also the point where one should exercise their right to choose. I totally believe that there is somebody for everybody. There are people who are compassionate, and patient enough to stand by the side of a loved one who suffers with mental illness. It's certainly a selfless and loving choice.

RED FLAGS show up in many ways.

Here are a few to pay close attention to and make wise decisions as needed:

- A Controlling nature or behavior
- Abusive or strong physical mishandling

- Lack of communication—Not much conversation
- Lack of Trust—continuous questioning of you or your whereabouts
- Unpredictable
- Immature
- Irresponsible
- Disliked by family and friends
- Signs of insecurity
- Unresolved past relationships
- Always pushing the boundaries
- Extremely High or low sex drive
- The push to separate or drive a wedge between family and friends
- Rushing a new relationship too quickly
- Overly enthused with you—you are excessively PERFECT in their eyes
- They belittle you in simple disagreement with name calling
- No work ethic
- No respect for their parents
- Extremely moody and constant change in attitude
- Habitual liar – dishonest about the small things
- Financial values differ from yours—spend thrift vs saver
- You are a secret

This is an extensive list.

Please don't ignore it. It could save your life.

…and your SANITY!

LOVE LESSON 7
Before Saying I Do
There's Still time to say, I Don't

I recently read that 20 percent of engagements are called off just before the wedding date. We've seen the movies like, "Run Away Bride", etc. The truth is, there are some situations that would require you to definitely put on a pair of your best Nike's or Reeboks and do a Flo jo! Run like crazy! However, take a long breath before making a drastic decision; and this is coming from the LovePreneuer.

As we've discussed in chapters 1 through 6, there are many, many factors to take into consideration BEFORE SAYING I DO. My hope is that, if you are embarking upon the world of marital bliss, that you would consider the key points FIRST before making a life changing decision. Marriage is such a beautiful commitment to love. It's the one thing that seals the deal for the love that so many speak and sing about. But it can also be the one thing, that makes others run the opposite way of true commitment and loyalty in a relationship.

If you are seriously planning the next step in your relationship, I beg of you to consider those subjects discussed that you resonate with you deep inside. In my 3 marriages, I had very high hope, and very high expectations. Had I taken account of these key points prior to saying "I DO", a lot of pain could have been avoided. Not to mention time and money; (just keeping it real). But the most important factor is SELF WORTH. Knowing "Thyself" is undervalued. One can say that they are a confident person, and that they have strong self-esteem. But until you hit that place where you are faced with some challenges that leave you dumb founded, speechless, or broken- hearted, you never really know your next step or move.

IT'S OKAY TO CHANGE YOUR MIND

No matter how much time spent on planning, effort (and money!). It is OK to change your mind. It's your life. It's your future, your peace of mind, and your self-worth. I like to give real life examples because they are reminders that 1) it happens and 2) you can survive it.

A very close and dear friend of mine had waited all of her life, for her prince charming. She met him. They fell in love. He proposed. She started planning THEEE WEDDING of the year. During this time, she had feelings of uncertainty. No one knew. But She knew what she had experienced with her fiancé. And she was the only one who mattered. No matter how excited we were for her big day, no matter how much money we spent to be a part of her big day; she became OUR SHERO the day she made a decision to cancel her wedding. My heart hurt for her because I knew how much she wanted marriage, and everything that came along with it. But my admiration for her went up by 10-fold!

See. If "she" –a woman who waited til middle age to marry, with no children, chose to say N-O because of significant reasons, then there was no choice, but to honor her decision, and her right to say, "I DON'T".

I'm a firm believer that whatever God has written your name on, will be delivered directly to you. Just like the post office. Sometimes your package may not come when you expect it. It may not be delivered in the original packaging. It may even come to you a little scuffed or damaged. But on the inside of that package is something SPECIAL. Something UNIQUE, something designed JUST FOR YOU. I encourage you to wait patiently on God. I recall being impatient many times. Making quick and hurried decisions. Which is why I had THREE HUSBANDS. Friend--- choose wisely. More importantly, allow God to choose for you. These 7 chapters were written with YOU in mind. I experienced a lot of pain, hurt, deception, and unrest. But through all of it, I asked God to show me the nuggets. And He gave me Diamonds instead.

This book title came from a cry of pain while begging God to help my hurt. A friend of mine (Amanda) spoke a powerful message recently at an empowerment brunch I hosted. She simply reminded the women in the room to turn your PAIN into POWER. Little did she know, that's exactly what I was doing. I encourage you to do the same. It works!

I recently attended the beloved ESSENCE Festival 2019. Former First Lady Michelle Obama spoke at the Mercedes Benz Dome, New Orleans. I was so excited to be in the building with beautiful women of all shades. It was so uplifting and inspiring to be amongst women of influence, women with aspirations, and women of POWER. In her candid conversation with Ms. Gayle King, she speaks of her experience with marriage. Here are a few notes that I took, that I couldn't wait to share with each of you.

Mrs. OBAMA said:

[SOURCE: quotes taken from notes from live candid conversation with Gayle King during the ESSENCE Festival 2019]

"Pick your mate like you would pick your team. You want a winning team. Not someone weak. Marry someone who is your equal. You don't someone who is not trustworthy. You want someone who has a heart for you and who will keep their word. The reason it's important to find someone and be with someone you love, and trust is because in the end, it's just you two. You need that. Don't let the way they chew and breathe aggravate you. Share the same values. Honesty. Truth. Resentment is toxic. Have balance No one can have it all.... especially at one time. Balance is the key. "

Song of Solomon 2; 16 (kjv)
"My beloved is mine, and I am his...."

My Three Husbands

Another great person that I admire, offers a few pieces of wisdom as it relates to marriage. Billionaire Warren Buffet advises:

[SOURCE: quotes taken from a CNBC published article]

"The biggest decision of your life is who you choose to marry. You want to associate with an individual who is the kind of person you'd like to be. You'll move in that direction. And the most important person by far in that respect is your spouse.

"Marry the right person. I'm serious about that. It will make more difference in your life. It will change your aspirations, all kinds of things"

Love is a beautiful union that God ordained. Choose wisely. And please remember that marriage is a 3 strand cord.

Ecclesiastes 4:12 (kjv)
"A cord of three strands is not quickly broken."

Best Wishes to all of the Future Mr. & Mrs.!

Kelly

www.ingramcontent.com/pod-product-compliance
Lightning Source LLC
Chambersburg PA
CBHW070032110426
42741CB00035B/2740